Simple Solutions

Senior Dogs

By
Kim Campbell Thornton
Illustrations by Buck Jones

With Health and Training Tips

BOWTIE
P R E S S ®

A Division of BowTie, Inc.
Irvine, California

Karla Austin, *Business Operations Manager*
Nick Clemente, *Special Consultant*
Kendra Strey, *Project Editor*
Susan Chaney, *Consulting Editor*

Jill Dupont, *Production*
Allyn A. Salmond, *Design*
Michael V. Capozzi, *Cover and book design concept*

The dogs in this book are referred to as *he* and *she* in alternating chapters.

Library of Congress-in-Publication Data
Thornton, Kim Campbell.
  Senior dogs / by Kim Campbell Thornton ; illustrations by Buck Jones.
      p. cm. — (Simple solutions)
  ISBN 1-931993-72-6
  1. Dogs. 2. Dogs—Aging. 3. Dogs—Health. 4. Dogs—Diseases. 5. Veterinary geriatrics. I. Title. II. Series:
Simple solutions (Irvine, Calif.)

  SF427.T493 2006
  636.7'089'897—dc22

2005016365

BowTie Press®
A Division of BowTie, Inc.
3 Burroughs
Irvine, California 92618

Printed and bound in Singapore
10 9 8 7 6 5 4 3 2 1

Contents

When Is a Dog Old?

Aging occurs when the body starts to deteriorate faster than it can regenerate. Some of us can recall when it started happening to our bodies. Our memories became less sharp and our bodies became more prone to soreness and stiffness after exertion. The same thing happens to our dogs as they age. Dogs age at different rates, depending on their breed, their size, and the simple luck of the genetic draw. For instance, large dogs tend to age more rapidly than do small dogs; flat-faced breeds tend to

age more rapidly than do dogs with longer muzzles. Some dogs just have good genes when it comes to longevity, no matter what their breed or size. In general, though, a dog enters her senior years at age seven or eight. Giant breeds typically begin aging a little earlier, achieving senior status at five or six years. Toy breeds age a little later than average, entering their golden years at approximately nine or ten years.

Fortunately for dogs (and for the people who love them), advances in veterinary medicine and canine nutrition have greatly increased the canine life span; senior diets, new

medications, and ramps and other aids are available to improve their health and comfort. With lots of love and good care, dogs can live into their mid-teens, with a rare few reaching advanced ages of eighteen or nineteen years.

How do you know if your dog is starting to feel the effects of age? You'll probably notice that she moves a little more slowly when she gets up from a nap. The dog who once walked with a spring in her step now moves at a sedate stroll. Her muzzle is gray and her eyebrows sprout white hairs. She may gain or lose weight. Ask yourself the following questions:

- Is my dog drinking more water than usual?

- Has she recently gained or lost 10 percent or more of her body weight?

- Has her appetite increased or decreased significantly?

- Is her coat or skin dry, dull, or flaky?

- Does she have less energy or stamina than usual?

- Does she have accidents in the house for no apparent reason?

If the answer is yes to one or more of these questions, it's time to make an appointment with your veterinarian for a golden-age checkup.

The Geriatric Exam

The golden years make up between 30 and 40 percent of a dog's life. During these years, a dog's body is constantly changing; his metabolism slows and he may develop health problems that require you to adjust his diet and exercise in order for him to remain healthy. Dog owners can sense some changes just by observing their pets. However, aging animals have many internal changes that could lead to health problems that can be detected only by a professional through a physical examination and lab work.

Nonetheless, only about 14 percent of senior animals get regular health screenings as recommended by their veterinarians. That's a shame, because preventive care can not only extend your dog's life but also help reduce your veterinary expenses because you're more likely to catch health problems before they take a bite out of your wallet.

When your dog starts getting on in years, even if he appears to be healthy, take him to the veterinarian for a geriatric checkup. This physical exam and the accompanying lab work will establish your dog's current health status, a baseline against which he can be judged as he continues to age. A semiyearly checkup can uncover health problems, such as tumors or dental disease, when they're easier and less expensive to treat. A thorough geriatric exam includes a complete physical, lab tests, and an interview with your veterinarian about your dog's lifestyle.

Before you head to the clinic, you should prepare for the exam. The veterinarian will want to know about your dog's habits, environment, and diet. Be prepared to tell her how often your dog goes for walks or gets exercise, how much and what type of food he eats, and what treats he gets. Discuss your dog's behavioral changes, such as sleeping more or less or being more or less

friendly toward friends or strangers. Inspect your dog's body for lumps or other issues such as skin irritations, and check to see whether he has a limp. It's a good idea to take notes and to make a list of questions so you don't forget anything. The information you gather will help give your veterinarian a complete picture of your dog's health.

At the clinic, your veterinarian may start the exam by observing your dog as he walks. This allows her to evaluate the way he moves, his apparent comfort level, and his overall body condition. She'll also check the dog's vital signs—temperature, heart rate and rhythm, and respiration—as well as his weight, reflexes, and hydration level. She'll run her hands over his abdomen to check the size and shape of the kidneys and liver. She'll feel for lumps on his body and search for signs of problems such as enlarged lymph glands or a subtle flinch that indicates pain. She'll test his range of motion by moving and bending his legs. The exam also includes vision and hearing checks; an evaluation of his coat, skin, toenails, and nail beds; and a look inside the mouth to see if he has bad breath, tartar on the teeth, or sores in the oral cavity.

Lab work may include a complete blood count (CBC), urinalysis, and fecal exam. Additional blood work will test such things as your dog's levels of blood urea nitrate (BUN) and creatinine, which are important in determining kidney health; glucose, high levels of which can indicate diabetes; and albumin, alkaline phosphatase, and bilirubin, which are indicators of liver function. Depending on your dog's medical history and the results of the exam and lab work, your veterinarian may also recommend diagnostic tests such as radiographs (X rays); an echocardiogram and an electrocardiogram (ECG or EKG) to assess heart function; a tear test for dry eye; or tonometry, a procedure that measures eye pressure and can indicate the presence of glaucoma (abnormally high eye pressure that could lead to blindness).

Now your veterinarian can take all this information and work with you to devise a lifestyle plan that will carry your dog through his senior years. In the following chapters, you'll find out how to recognize common health ailments and what changes you can make to your dog's feeding and activity routines to make him as comfortable as possible in his golden years.

Age-Related Health Problems

Common problems in aging dogs include arthritis, cancer, dental disease, eye disease, hearing loss, heart disease, hypothyroidism, kidney disease, and senility. Although some of these problems are for the most part unavoidable, you can take steps to treat them or reduce their severity, especially if they're detected in the early stages. Others, such as diabetes, are exacerbated by obesity, so keeping your dog at a healthy weight throughout her life can help ward off this disease. If you purchased your dog from a breeder, find out what health problems affected your dog's parents and grandparents and how old they were at the time. This will help you

know what to expect or even allow you to take preventive steps, if possible.

Arthritis. If your dog seems stiff after standing up or is reluctant to go up or down stairs, jump on or off furniture, or climb in or out of the car, she may have arthritis. This painful joint disease affects an estimated 70 to 80 percent of dogs of certain breeds. Most prone to arthritis are large breeds such as golden retrievers, Labrador retrievers, German shepherd dogs, Newfoundlands, and Saint Bernards; especially susceptible is a large breed dog who a veterinarian determines has excessive laxity, or looseness, in the hip joints. Nonetheless, any dog—large or small—can develop

arthritis, and it is most common in dogs age seven and older.

Medication in the form of nonsteroidal anti-inflammatory

drugs (NSAIDs) is available to treat arthritis pain. Be aware that while NSAIDs have significantly helped many dogs, there are some dogs who

are sensitive to these drugs and may experience serious or even fatal side effects. Responsible veterinarians require dogs on NSAIDs to have blood tests every three to six months to make sure the drugs aren't having any adverse effects on the liver and kidneys. Ask your veterinarian about the potential side effects of any drug prescribed so you'll know what to watch for.

Although it hasn't been proven scientifically, arthritis may also be helped by nutraceuticals—foods or nutritional supplements with health benefits—such as glucosamine and chondroitin, which help to repair cartilage and may reduce pain and inflammation. These supplements have no side effects or only minor side effects and can be purchased in pet supply stores. Ask your veterinarian about the appropriate amount to give your dog. A number of dog foods and treats also contain these supplements. Other complementary therapies that may help relieve arthritis pain are acupuncture, chiropractic, and massage.

Cancer. Cancer is the uncontrolled growth of cells on or in the body. The incidence of cancer increases with age; dogs age ten or older are most likely to develop cancer.

Not surprisingly, cancer is the most common cause of death in dogs. The good news is that it's more treatable now than it has ever been, especially if it's detected in the early stages.

Dogs can develop benign or malignant tumors. Benign tumors are harmless and noninvasive, meaning they don't spread to other areas of the body. Malignant tumors are harmful; they invade surrounding tissues and can spread to other areas of the body via the bloodstream or lymph system. The most common malignant cancers in dogs are lymphoma (lymphoid tissues), osteosarcoma (bones), soft

tissue sarcomas (muscles and connective tissues), oral melanoma (mouth), and mammary cancer (chest area).

Be aware of and watch for the ten warning signs of cancer: unusual swellings that don't go away or that grow in size; sores that don't heal; unexplained weight loss; loss of appetite; bleeding or discharge from any body opening such as the mouth, nose, or anus; an unexplained bad smell coming from the body; difficulty eating or swallowing; hesitation to exercise or a loss of stamina; persistent lameness or stiffness; or difficulty breathing, urinating, or defecating.

If you notice any of these signs in your dog, take her to the veterinarian. Cancer can be diagnosed through a physical exam, radiographs, blood tests, and in some cases a surgical biopsy in which a sample of tissue is removed for study. If necessary, your veterinarian can refer you to a board-certified veterinary oncologist for diagnosis and treatment. Depending on the type of cancer, it may be treated with surgery, chemotherapy, radiation, or a combination of these methods. Researchers are studying ways to kill cancers by cutting off the blood supply to the tumor.

Dental Disease. Dental disease is a common and serious problem in older dogs. Unbrushed teeth are a breeding ground for bacteria, and plaque and tartar buildup on teeth

can cause them to hurt. If your dog is picking up her food and then dropping it, she may have painful dental disease.

Brushing her teeth at home and scheduling yearly (at least) professional teeth cleaning with your veterinarian will help keep dental disease at bay. Even if you haven't been brushing her teeth, it's never too late to start. After she's had a good veterinary cleaning to scrape off the ugly brown buildup, begin a consistent daily (or at least weekly) brushing routine at home. Brushing and professional cleanings help keep gums and teeth healthy and prevent bacteria from entering the bloodstream and spreading to other organs in the body, such as the heart and kidneys.

Eye Disease. Cataracts, dry eye, and nuclear sclerosis are all forms of eye disease that can affect aging dogs. Fortunately, most dogs get along just fine with a decrease in or even complete loss of their eyesight. They can run, play, and even hunt without their vision simply by making better use of their senses of hearing and smell. The better news is that, in many cases, canine eye problems are treatable with medication or with surgery.

Your dog may have cataracts if one or both of her eyes look cloudy. A cataract is a clouding of the lens of the eye or its surrounding transparent membrane; the condition will gradually progress until vision is lost. Cataracts can be removed with a machine that uses ultrasonic sound waves to break down and remove the lens from the eye. A synthetic eye lens is then surgically implanted. Most dogs will develop cataracts in both eyes, and it's less expensive to have the surgery done on both eyes at the same appointment. As with most health problems, the success rate is greatest when cataracts are noticed and treated early. If surgery isn't an option for financial reasons, be aware that cataracts can eventually cause inflammation as they worsen. When this is the case, your dog may need medication periodically for the rest of her life.

Sometimes mistaken for cataracts, nuclear sclerosis is the most benign of the eye problems that affect old dogs. As dogs age, the lenses of their eyes harden and develop a hazy grayish appearance. Nuclear sclerosis is a normal part of aging and doesn't affect vision.

Older dogs can also develop dry eye (formally, keratoconjunctivitis sicca). Dry eye occurs when the tear glands can't produce enough moisture for the cornea, which results in redness, cloudiness, thick discharge, and frequent eye infections. It's especially common in small breeds, such as Lhasa apsos, pugs, and shih tzu, but a number of other breeds can also be predisposed to it. After diagnosing dry eye with a Schirmer tear test, which measures tear production, your veterinarian can prescribe medication to stimulate tears, as well as prescribe artificial tears, antibiotics, and anti-inflammatory drugs as needed.

Hearing Loss. Your old dog isn't always ignoring you when she doesn't respond to your call. She may not be able to hear you. Ears, like other organs, can lose their acuity with age, either because of a history of ear infections or simply because the sound receptors in the

ear have begun to degenerate. There's not much you can do for deafness, but you can still communicate with your dog. Teach her hand signals for basic commands such as *sit*, *down*, and *stay*. When she's lying down or sleeping and you want to alert her to your presence, stomp your foot. She'll feel the vibrations and know you're nearby.

Heart Disease. As dogs age, their heart functions may begin to deteriorate. Consider this possibility if your older dog is suddenly less able to tolerate even small amounts of exercise, if she coughs for no apparent reason, or if her gums or tongue appear bluish instead of a healthy pink.

Your veterinarian can often hear a heart murmur (an abnormal rhythm) with a stethoscope, but X rays, an ultrasound, and an electrocardiogram are necessary to determine the extent of the problem. Medication and sometimes diet can help control certain heart problems for a time.

Hypothyroidism. This is a common hormonal disorder that most often affects middle-aged and senior dogs. As dogs age, their levels of thyroid hormone can decrease, causing skin and coat problems—such as hair loss, slow regrowth, and overall coat dullness—unexplained weight gain, lethargy, and mental dullness. Hypothyroidism is diagnosed with a blood test that measures the level of circulating thyroid hormone. It's easily treated with a daily dose of synthetic thyroid hormone, given in the form of a pill.

Kidney Disease. Kidney failure is one of the most common causes of death in older dogs. The kidneys are multitaskers; they filter waste from the body and eliminate it as urine, they maintain the balance of chemicals in the blood, they help regulate blood pressure, and they produce erythropoietin— a hormone that stimulates the production of red blood cells. When the kidneys begin to fail—a process that can take months or years—toxins build up in the blood. Kidney failure can be far advanced by the time it's discovered, which is one of the many reasons semiyearly geriatric exams are important. When detected early, kidney disease can be kept at bay with an appropriate diet and in some cases medication and IV fluid therapy. Vitamin B, C, and E supplements, and omega-3 fatty acid supplements can also help. If your dog has kidney disease, be sure she always has plenty of fresh water available.

Senility. Yes, dogs can become senile as they age, a condition formally called cognitive dysfunction syndrome (CDS). It's caused by degenerative changes in the brain. Signs of CDS in dogs include anxiety, confusion, aimless wandering, house-training accidents, irritability, less desire to interact with people, changes in sleep habits, and

repetitive behaviors or changes in activity level. Don't assume that nothing can be done if your older dog seems to have lost her way mentally. The signs of CDS can be managed with medication, environmental changes, and behavior modification techniques, such as revisiting basic house-training. First, though, CDS must be correctly diagnosed, because some of these signs can be caused by other health problems, such as arthritis, heart disease, hormonal disorders, or urinary tract infections. Several medications and even a special diet prescribed by your veterinarian can help if CDS is indeed the problem.

Be Prepared. Our pets are living longer lives thanks to better care and nutrition. Since the majority of veterinary expenses occur in an animal's senior years, today's pet owners face a longer period of time in which these costs add up. Consider purchasing pet health insurance. Some companies offer policies designed with senior dogs in mind. If you'd rather not shell out a monthly payment, start saving when your pet's still a pup so you're prepared for future expenses. By setting aside money throughout her life, you'll have money available to help pay for treatment when it's most needed.

A Comfortable Old Age

As your dog grows older, he will slow down, but that doesn't mean he can't still enjoy life. It's easy to make changes that will help him stay comfortable and remain able to participate in family activities. Here are some ways to make his life easier.

Provide a comfortable bed in a warm place. You can purchase an orthopedic bed designed to cushion and warm rickety bones; a simple fleece throw in a favorite sunny spot works, too. Place a nonskid mat beneath the bed or throw so your dog doesn't slip and hurt himself. Put several cushy beds around the house so your dog always has a comfy place to rest. Especially nice during winter are discs, wraps, or pads designed to be heated in

the microwave; when placed in or on your dog's bedding, these devices give off warmth for several hours.

Warmth is soothing to achy joints, but extreme

temperatures (whether hot or cold) are hard on older dogs. Keep them in air-conditioned comfort during the heat of the day, and limit walks to cool mornings and evenings. This is especially important for flat-faced breeds such as boxers, bulldogs, Pekingese, and pugs, because they can develop respiratory problems if they exert themselves in the heat. You may also want to purchase a doggy water bed to help your dog stay cool during summertime.

Buy or build a sturdy ramp or step to help your dog climb onto the bed or sofa—assuming he's allowed there—

or into the car. You can help dogs with weak rear ends walk or climb stairs by holding a towel beneath their bellies (behind their rib cages) and pulling upward to give support. If you have a small dog (or a strong back and biceps), simply lift your dog on and off furniture and in and out of the car. You'll help save his joints from excess stress.

Slick wood or tile floors can cause old dogs to slip and fall. Lay carpet runners through your home's main walkways to provide sure footing.

If your dog's eyesight has gone dim, refrain from moving household furniture around unless it's absolutely necessary. Create a scent trail to help him navigate around furniture; at his nose level, mark couches and such with perfume or some other scent. Don't forget to test whatever you use as a scent in an inconspicuous area to make sure it doesn't mar your furniture. Another way to accommodate dogs who have lost their vision is to use toys with

bells on them. When you toss the toy, the dog can follow

the sound of the bell to retrieve it. You can attach small

bells to toys yourself if you have sewing skills, or you can look for toys with bells or other noisemakers at the pet supply store. When playing or just spending time outdoors, keep him leashed or confine him to a fenced yard for protection from street traffic and yard hazards.

Your older dog's bladder doesn't have the holding capacity it used to. Take him out to eliminate more often, or make sure he has access to the yard through a dog door. Or, ask a neighbor or hire a pet sitter to drop by and take him out. Another alternative is to confine your home alone dog to a room that has tile or vinyl flooring, which isn't as difficult to clean as is carpet. Reward him when he potties outdoors.

A female dog who has been spayed sometimes "leaks" urine during her senior years. You may notice a small damp spot on her bedding after she gets up in the morning. Don't scold her; instead, ask your veterinarian to prescribe a medication that can help control her bladder. You can also purchase canine diapers to keep leaks contained. It's also a good idea to have your veterinarian check for a bladder infection or kidney dysfunction.

Pay attention to how your dog uses his dog door. Arthritis or other orthopedic problems may make it difficult for him to pass through it as easily as he once did. You may need to

adjust the height or width of the door. Don't forget to provide secure footing on both sides of the door.

Some dogs develop separation anxiety with age. Others become what we might call senile, often forgetting where they are or becoming anxious at certain hours, such as nightfall. Leaving the radio or the television on at a low level may help them remain calm.

Health, Diet, and Grooming

Take your dog in for a veterinary once-over every six months instead of the annual exams she had during her first five or so years. Keep in mind that dogs age five to seven years for every calendar year that passes, so health problems can develop more rapidly than you might expect.

Keep her weight at a normal level. Excess weight puts pressure on joints, which can worsen arthritis. Obesity also increases a dog's risk of developing health problems such as diabetes and heart disease. If your older dog is putting on weight, cut back on her food portions, switch her to a low-calorie diet, or add fiber to her meals in the form of rinsed canned green beans or unsweetened canned pumpkin. The extra fiber will help her feel full.

Bathe and brush her regularly checking her entire body for lumps and bumps that could indicate tumors. Many older dogs develop harmless bumps on or beneath the skin, but sometimes they're a warning sign of cancer. Have your veterinarian check out these bumps, especially if they seem to be growing rapidly or changing shape or color.

Keep toenails trimmed so they don't catch on carpets or cause your dog to fall on slick floors.

Keep up the parasite control efforts. Older dogs have less resistance to diseases carried by blood-sucking parasites such as fleas, ticks, and intestinal worms.

Activity Level and Mental Stimulation

Continue providing exercise. Your dog might not be able to jog with you anymore, but he can still enjoy a leisurely walk. If it's hard for you to walk at a slow pace, tote him along in a wagon or jogging stroller while you run so he still gets the stimulation of being outdoors and seeing other people and animals.

Walking isn't the only way your dog can exercise. If you have a water-loving dog, swimming is a great way for him to get some non-weight-bearing exercise, which is easier on his joints

than walking on hard pavement. Limit swimming to summertime, though, unless you have access to a heated, indoor physical therapy pool for dogs; older dogs are sensitive to extreme temperatures (cold or hot), and you don't want him to catch a chill.

Mental exercise is just as important for your dog as physical exercise is. Take him for a car ride, run him through some simple obedience exercises, or let him take part in an activity from his past, such as showing in the Veterans Class at a dog show.

What's the most important thing you can do for your older dog? Love him. Now, more than ever, he needs your attention, affection, and sweet talk. Cherish these golden years so that when he's gone, your tears will be tempered with memories of the good times.

Kim Campbell Thornton is an award-winning writer and editor. During her tenure as editor of *Dog Fancy*, the magazine won three Dog Writers Association of America Maxwell Awards for best all-breed magazine. Her book *Why Do Cats Do That?* was named best behavior book in 1997 by the Cat Writers Association. Kim is the author of the Simple Solutions™ series books *Barking*, *Chewing*, *Digging*, *House-Training*, and *Aggression*. She is also the former president of the Cat Writers Association.

Buck Jones' humorous illustrations have appeared in numerous magazines (including *Dog Fancy* and *Cat Fancy*) and books. He is the illustrator for the best-selling Simple Solutions series books, *Why Do Cockatiels Do That?*, *Why Do Parakeets Do That?*, *Kittens! Why Do They Do What They Do?*, and *Puppies! Why Do They Do What They Do?* Contact Buck through his Web site: http://www.buckjonesillustrator.com.